Anthropologist: Scientist of the People

ANTHROPOLOGIST:
SCIENTIST OF THE PEOPLE

Mary Batten

~: with photographs by A. Magdalena Hurtado and Kim Hill

HOUGHTON MIFFLIN COMPANY

BOSTON 2001

To the Aché and all other hunter-gatherers who still survive, with profound thanks for all that you teach us about what it means to be human

ACKNOWLEDGMENTS

We thank Sarah Blaffer Hrdy for bringing us together to work on this book. Her work has always been inspirational to us, and we designate her the "godmother" of this book.

A. M. H. and K. H. thank the families of Martin Achipuragi, Chito Membogi, Antonio Kuachigi, Carlos Kanewatapegi, Felipe Jakugi, Roberto Tykuanagi, Carlos Bejywagi, Ambrocho Bepuragi, Tito Tykuanagi, Enrique Tykuanagi, and Margarita Bywagi. They also thank Hillard Kaplan, Raúl Gauto, Alberto Yanosky, Nancy Cardozo, Alberto Madroño, Rosalino and Nati Vega, Bjarne and Rosalba Fostervold, Lucy Aquino, John Wickman, Tim McCall, John McCall, Dolly Smith, and the park guards of the Mbaracayú Reserve.

M. B. is profoundly grateful to Magdalena Hurtado for sharing her life and work. Without her close collaboration, friendship, and trust, this book could not have been written. M. B. also thanks Kim Hill and Beth Pickett, who read the entire manuscript and made many helpful comments; her agent, Barbara Markowitz, and Harvey Markowitz, for their ongoing assistance; and her husband, Ed Bland, for his continuing encouragement and support.

Last, but certainly not least, we thank our editor, Amy Flynn, whose insightful comments helped to give this book its final form and polish.

THE FOREST

∵ "I love sleeping in the forest. There is a sense of safety that is so wonderful, because you're with people who are such masters of the forest."

I**T IS BARELY DAWN** when the forest birds begin singing. The kuachi beats its wings and makes a rough sound, trrrrrrrr-trrrrrrrr, that can be heard far away. The kuato sings a deep, almost sorrowful song, auUU, auUU. Nearby along the riverbank, frogs are still chorusing. Slowly, the muted sounds of the night give way to the laughterlike squawks of the peta, a loudmouthed bird that wakes up everyone.

Anthropologist Magdalena Hurtado opens her eyes and lies quietly, enjoying the soft whispers of people awakening around her. There are about twenty-five people—mothers, fathers, children, aunts, uncles, grandparents, cousins, and friends. They have all slept on the ground inside the dense tropical forest of the Mbaracayú Reserve in Paraguay, a country in South America. Although she is many miles from the nearest town, Magdalena feels safe. She is surrounded by people she has known and studied for many years, people who are now her close friends. She is on a foraging trip with a group of hunter-gatherers called the Aché (ah-CHAY), and this is the way each day begins.

In the gray morning light, the men move as softly as shadows. Using snail shells from the forest floor, they rub their arrow tips, sharpening them as they prepare for the day's

~: The Aché find all they need to live in the forest. Men make bows and arrows out of palm wood. Women carry the family's belongings in a basket that they weave from palm leaves.

hunt. The women break sticks and light fires to take away the morning chill. The children are hungry. Everyone is hungry, but they know there will be no big meal until evening. They make a breakfast of food left over from the night before and nearby fruits.

The men gather their bows and arrows and go deeper into the forest to hunt. With machetes, they cut a trail for the women and children to follow. The women look for ripe fruit or insect larvae to eat. At the end of the day, they will set up camp and cook the animals the men have killed. Then they share all the food with their families and friends so that everyone has something to eat.

This is the way the Aché live — each day on the move, hunting and gathering, depending on what their forest environment provides. Until the 1970s, the forest was the only home the Aché ever had. Now they live in small houses with wooden floors on reservations, where they face the difficult challenge of learning to farm. But many still return to the forest for weeks or months at a time to pursue their old way of life. It is here that Magdalena lives with them when she leaves her comfortable home and university teaching job in the United States and goes into the field to work with the Aché and study their culture.

The Aché are among the few hunter-gatherer groups left in the world. Others live in South America, Africa, and Asia, but not all hunter-gatherers are alike. Each group has its own distinct culture. Magdalena has lived with tribes like the Machiguenga, who inhabit such a remote area of the Amazon rainforest that she was the first white woman they had ever seen. There are people living deep in South America's rainforests who have still never had contact with the outside world.

We know about the Aché and other hunter-gatherers through the work of anthropologists like Magdalena. An anthropologist is a scientist who studies people. Anthropology

~: Magdalena's head makes a soft perch for a pet capuchin monkey. The Aché love pets and adopt monkeys and other forest animals.

comes from two Greek words: *anthropos*, which means "human being," and *logy*, which means "a field of science."

Magdalena is the kind of anthropologist called a human evolutionary ecologist. She uses the science of evolutionary biology to study people, just as biologists use this same science to study animals. Evolutionary biology teaches that all animals, including people, do whatever is necessary in a particular environment to survive, mate, and bear healthy offspring that will in turn survive, mate, and reproduce. Although individuals in different animal species and in different human societies have various ways of doing these things, they are all trying to survive and reproduce successfully.

Anthropologists like Magdalena ask "why" questions: Why do people spend as much time foraging as they do? Why do they like to eat some animals and plants but not others? Why do men and women do different kinds of work? Why is finding a mate so important? Why do people care more for some sick individuals than others? Why do people in hunter-gatherer societies share more food than do members of other societies? Why are many indigenous people free of health problems such as asthma and diabetes?

The answers to these kinds of questions help to explain a society's social organization, customs, and myths. For example,

in just about every society—from hunter-gatherers to our own—women prefer to mate with men who have resources. This is because women invest more of their biology in bearing and caring for babies than men do. Women want a mate who can help them feed, protect, and take care of their children. So men in most cultures display their resources and compete with one another to attract mates. Among hunter-gatherers, food is a major resource and survival depends on skill in finding it. So among the Aché, women are attracted to strong, successful hunters.

In the forest with the Aché, Magdalena experiences human nature as close to the rest of nature as it is possible to be. She learns firsthand how people forage for food and live off the land—a way of life that all humans pursued for hundreds of thousands of years, before the wheel or metal tools were invented and before there were farms, villages, or cities. All of

☙ Left: The bill of a toucan, a large forest bird, is a tool used to apply glue to an arrow. The glue is made from beeswax mixed with charcoal. Right: Aché men gather honeycomb with their bare hands. Sometimes they get stung.

~: Vijulla fruit, which tastes like grapes, is a favorite snack.

us alive today are descended from hunter-gatherers. Although our way of life is far removed from theirs, our biology, many of our behaviors, and some of our cravings have been shaped by an ancient past.

For example, just about everybody loves to eat sweets. For hunter-gatherers, a sweet taste means fruit is ripe and ready to eat. A "sweet tooth" probably evolved many thousands of years ago as foraging peoples learned to avoid bitter tastes, which are associated with plant toxins that might make them sick or even kill them.

Similarly, most people like fatty foods. Fat, which supplies a lot of calories and energy, was probably in short supply among our hunter-gatherer ancestors. Unlike modern people who overeat fats and sweets, which are readily available, hunter-gatherers probably never had too much of this kind of food.

For the Aché, the forest is their supermarket, pharmacy, and home. They know the forest as well as a city dweller knows the streets.

Although the Aché live very different lives than we do, they are like us in many ways. They have feelings and concerns that all other human beings share: love, happiness, excitement, anger, fear, pain, and sadness. Birth and death mark the lives of all of us, no matter where or how we live.

BECOMING AN ANTHROPOLOGIST

✥ "To be an anthropologist, you have to be so interested in people that you can sit in a hut for hours without being bored."

MAGDALENA HAS ALWAYS been fascinated by different kinds of people. Her mother, Ines, a medical doctor, is from Colombia. Her father, Luis, a real estate appraiser, is from the area of southern France near the Spanish border.

The youngest of five children, Madgalena grew up in a small community of professional people near Caracas, the capital city of Venezuela. Several adults in the community were scientists who worked at a research institute. Her parents, along with others in the community, organized the school that Magdalena and other children attended. Scientists came and spoke to their classes. Anthropologists visited her home, and her mother took her to every anthropological exhibit in the area.

From earliest childhood, Magdalena was exposed to all kinds of people. Sometimes her mother took her along when she went into the rural coffee-growing areas to provide free medical care to the peasants, who lived in great poverty. Those visits made a lasting impression on Magdalena. She saw babies dying and people suffering from horrible wounds. She

✥ The future anthropologist, age one and a half years.

: Magdalena grew up near Caracas, Venezuela.

watched how her mother showed respect and compassion for her patients.

Sometimes her mother went on expeditions with scientists to remote areas where she met indigenous people—native people who originated in a particular region. She returned home with handmade baskets, tools, and other artifacts that Magdalena found both strange and beautiful. She was also impressed by the beautiful photographs that her father had taken of the Cuna Indians when he worked for the Panamanian government in the early 1940s. "I had the idea that anthropology was just the coolest thing to do," Magdalena says. "My mother and father had such admiration for people of different cultures."

Magdalena's parents taught her that it was important to be a citizen of the world. They also taught her one of a scientist's basic skills: asking questions. "Questioning everything has been the whole theme of my life," Magdalena says. "I started out asking questions about a lot of things. I had to ask questions about every single thing I was ever taught. I wanted to know, Is there anything universal about what you're teaching me? I didn't call it anthropology; it was just a personal quest."

Originally, Magdalena wanted to become an educator, but when she discovered how ethnocentric—focused on one country or one ethnic group—educational systems tend to be, she decided to go into anthropology.

When she is not in the field working with the Aché, she is teaching anthropology students at the University of New Mexico in Albuquerque. From the continual questioning that marked her childhood, Magdalena became a scientist.

A scientist asks a question and then designs an experiment or collects observations that will provide answers. But designing an experiment in the laboratory is very different from conducting a study in the field.

When working with people in the field, an anthropologist has to ask questions that can be answered without offending the people being studied. "You want to get the biggest bang out of what you're doing," says Magdalena, "so you try to ask questions that will tell a lot about human evolution and social organization." For example, why do women prefer certain men over others as mates?

∿ Magdalena is the youngest in her family. Top, from left to right: Montserrat, mother Ines, Jorge; bottom, from left to right: José Carlos, baby Magdalena, and Pablo.

At the beginning of her career, Magdalena realized that an anthropologist has both an enormous privilege and an enormous responsibility. "You're essentially bothering a group of people. Your presence is intrusive, and out of respect for the people, you have to make sure that whatever you're doing is really worthwhile. Nobody ever taught me anything about this in anthropology classes, but I think it's at the crux of anthropological research."

Magdalena first met the Aché in September 1981 through her husband, Kim Hill, also an anthropologist. She was twenty-four years old then, and she remembers the first meeting as if it happened yesterday. "People come to you and they try to figure out where you came

~ Magdalena and Kim use their motorcycle to travel places their truck can't reach.

from. They touch you, and there's all this body language that's so different from what we see in other cultures. I love the physical interaction, and I go along with it. I immediately make friends. It's wonderful; I don't have to speak the language."

Learning the language of the people is one of the most difficult skills an anthropologist has to master, but it is absolutely essential to fieldwork. Despite all its difficulties, Magdalena had confidence that she could learn Aché. After all, she had overcome a far more difficult language problem when she had to learn English.

When she was twelve years old, her family moved from Venezuela to New York City, where her mother had a fellowship to get her Ph.D. in immunology, the science of how the body fights disease. Suddenly, Magdalena found herself in the seventh grade in a New York City public school, and she spoke no English. "Moving to New York was one of the most traumatic experiences of my life," she says.

Struggling to learn English, Magdalena often said the wrong thing and was very embarrassed. Other children made fun of her, but by the end of her first year in New York she had learned enough to keep up and pass her grade with high marks. To learn Aché, she used the same tricks that she had used to teach herself English. She learned key phrases, pointed to objects and asked people how to say the words for them, mimicked what people said, and wrote down everything. She let the people who spoke the language help teach her. The children especially helped her learn Aché. In the field, Magdalena wrote down every new Aché word in the little notebook she wore around her neck. She also recorded her observations as she carried out her studies. Just as other scientists enter their observations, or data, in a computer, Magdalena used her notebook as a database. In fact, she still uses notebooks, because laptop computers are unreliable in humid and dusty climates. She has had several laptops stop working within a few months of arriving in the field.

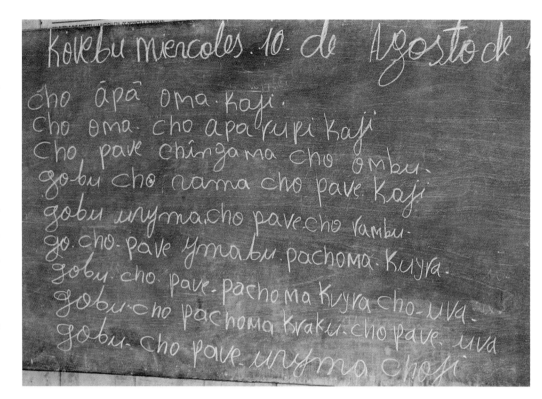

SCIENCE IN THE FIELD

There are certain methods that Magdalena and other anthropologists use to study people in the field. One technique is called focal follow. This means that each morning, as soon as she opens her eyes, Magdalena randomly picks a woman that she will follow all day long. Throughout the day, she writes in her notebook everything that the woman does. She picks a different woman every day until she has collected information on every woman in the group.

Information gathered day after day makes the notebooks quite valuable. Magdalena, Kim, and the student researchers they sometimes take into the field worry constantly about losing their notebooks or getting them wet and having the ink run. To protect the notebooks, they keep them in plastic bags. One day, Magdalena lost her notebook. When she told one of the Aché women what happened, they began walking back along the trail, looking everywhere

⌁ The Aché language is nothing like Magdalena's native language, Spanish. For a long time, the Aché had no written language, but, thanks to missionaries, there is now an Aché dictionary. The people have been learning to read and write their language for the last twenty years.

~: In the early years of their fieldwork, Magdalena and Kim lived in a tent. In 1987, a windstorm flattened the tent and broke the poles holding it up. Magdalena and Kim had to use wooden sticks to raise the tent again.

for it. Magdalena had just about given up hope of finding it when an old Aché man came up the trail holding her precious notebook.

A second technique for learning how people spend their time is called "scan sampling." When using this research method, Magdalena takes a census, or count, of everyone in the group at the first rest stop on a foraging trip. Then, every ten or fifteen minutes, when the timer on her watch goes off, she looks around and writes notes describing what everyone is doing at that particular time. Today, she and the other researchers have tape recorders and dictate their notes on cassettes.

When Magdalena leaves the field and returns to her office at the University of New Mexico, she organizes the data to see what patterns emerge. When she feels she has collected enough data to test scientific hypotheses or to describe the patterns she finds, she writes a paper that gets published in one of the scientific journals, such as *Human Ecology*.

During her many years working with the Aché, Magdalena has been particularly interested in women's lives and the differences between men's and women's work. The difference that interested her the most was why men hunt and women gather. Most indigenous societies have this sexual division of labor. But why? How did this division evolve? From her studies, Magdalena has learned that women who are nursing a baby spend less time foraging than do women without a baby. From her observations of Aché women, Magdalena has proposed an important hypothesis. She suggests that the sexual division of labor in the human species may have evolved when females ignored opportunities for hunting animals because doing so would reduce both the time women could spend mothering and the quality of that mothering. Reduced mothering would result in higher death rates of children. Magdalena is the first anthropologist who has measured and tested ideas that would help explain the sexual division of labor. She repeated her tests among various groups of hunter-gatherers. If other scientists accept Magdalena's conclusions, she will have greatly expanded our understanding of our species.

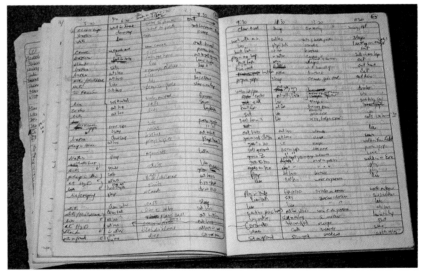

☙ Taking accurate notes is very important for good science. These notes are scan samples of daily activities.

✦ Aché mothers like Krajagi carry their babies everywhere.

Another important study that Magdalena and Kim have worked on together deals with the Aché's foraging behavior. To learn how much food value, or how many calories, the Aché get out of their hunting and gathering, Magdalena and Kim spent a lot of time weighing every item of food, no matter how small, brought into camp. With a portable spring scale, they weighed fruit, insect larvae, and animals. They also weighed pots of honey, making sure to subtract the weight of the pot from the total.

The Aché enjoyed the weighing, and some of the children learned how to use the scale.

Through the weighing study, Magdalena, Kim, and their students learned that Aché men and women are highly selective when they hunt and gather. They don't just kill or gather everything they find; rather, they go after animals, such as monkey, paca (a forest rodent), armadillo, deer, and peccary (wild pig), or plant products, like palm fruit, that provide the most calories for each hour they forage. People in the modern world would say that the Aché are very efficient at getting the most out of their work.

From the data they collected, Kim, Magdalena, and their colleagues who worked on the study have shown that the Aché eat very well, as much as 2,700 calories per person per day. This is more than many active American adults eat per day! Some people might find it surprising that the Aché eat so well, but the forest has an abundance of many kinds of food. Meat is very important to the Aché. Almost eighty percent of their calories come from animals; about ten percent comes from plants and insects, and honey makes up another ten percent.

↝ Magdalena's younger daughter, Daisha, helps collect samples of bacteria that cause sickness among the Aché.

DISCOVERING A PEOPLE'S HISTORY

Imagine trying to learn about the history of people who have no written history, no records of births, deaths, or marriages. This was the challenge that Magdalena and Kim faced in putting together a life history of the Aché. The first task was to gather details about the

🔅 Left: A young Membogi checks his arrow. Right: Now older, Membogi looks for monkey in the treetops.

Aché's past, which were stored in their memories. To gather these details, Magdalena and Kim interviewed every adult in their study group. Many individuals didn't know their age, so Magdalena and Kim had to think of a way to find out when people were born.

First, they asked older relatives to remember things from their past, such as their puberty ceremony. Kim and Magdalena asked: "Who was at the ceremony?" "Who was younger than you?" "Who was older than you?" Then they would ask an older person to tell when a younger person was born, and who else was born before and after that person.

After they had gotten all the older people's opinions about who was younger and who was older, Magdalena and Kim made a huge age chart that ranked individuals as older or younger. Then they tried to relate each person's birth year with a known, historical date for certain events. For example, they asked older people whether a particular individual was born when the road was being built. By conducting interviews and gathering many details, they were able to get a good idea of the year most individuals were born.

They also asked each man and woman how many children they had, whether any children had died,

~: Two generations, Jakugi and his son Wypygi.

and, if so, what the cause of death was. They asked each person about relatives, both living and dead. Through these interviews, Magdalena and Kim collected a detailed history of the Aché in their study group. Information about ages, births, and deaths of a population is called a demographic history. This kind of history is invaluable to anthropologists. It provides a big picture of family relationships, the age at which most men and women marry, when women give birth, how many children they have, how long most people live, birth and death rates, causes of death, and many other details that are important for understanding a society.

Many Aché enjoyed the interviews. When they realized that Magdalena and Kim could tape stories about their lives, they began talking more freely. "This is my speak," they would

‌ In her office, Magdalena analyzes their field data.

say as they described a hunting trip, a close call with a jaguar, or how a sister got killed. Sometimes they would cry while telling their stories.

When they returned to the University of New Mexico, Magdalena and Kim stored their data in a computer database. After fourteen years of collecting data, they used statistics to analyze it, and then spent about five years writing up the information they had gathered in a book about the Aché, *Aché Life History*. College students in anthropology read Kim and Magdalena's book to learn about the Aché and their quickly disappearing way of life.

LIVING WITH THE AÇHÉ

꙳ "There is something about living with the Aché that changed my life completely. From the very first day I was there, I had to let go of most things I ever believed in."

SINCE HER FIRST MEETING with the Aché in 1981, Magdalena has made many trips into the field. Almost every year since then, she has worked in the field for periods of time ranging from one to thirteen months. She and Kim have taken their two daughters, Karina and Daisha, with them since they were babies. For Magdalena, working in the field is very much a family affair, but it has never been easy. She, Kim, and their daughters have gotten sick with diarrhea because of the different bacteria and other organisms in the food and water. They have lost weight, had fevers, and suffered from insect bites. At night in the forest, Magdalena boils water and stores it in plastic containers. She has learned that as long as she drinks boiled water she will not get sick as often.

Magdalena's travel to reach the Aché is long and difficult. From the United States, she flies to Asunción, the capital city of Paraguay. Nowadays when she arrives in Asunción, she gets in a four-wheel-drive truck for the long trip to the research

꙳ Magdalena with Karina, age four. Their faces are painted with a dye made from a genipa fruit that the Aché call bellaprana.

25

BOLIVIA

BRAZIL

PARAGUAY

Mbaracayú Reserve

★Asunción

ARGENTINA

☙ The Mbaracayú Reserve covers 270 square miles, about four times the size of Washington, D.C.

headquarters she and Kim established for themselves and other researchers in the Mbaracayú Reserve. Depending on the conditions of the roads, the trip can take from nine hours to three days. They drive slowly for their safety because the dirt roads are bumpy and sometimes flooded during the rainy season. Even though it is slow, the truck is luxurious compared to the rickety old bus they used to ride during the early 1980s. Some of the buses had no windows, and the heat or cold, depending on the season of the year, was intense. Sometimes the bus was so crowded, Magdalena had to stand the entire way with her baby daughter, Karina.

Although this part of the world is warm and wet most of the year, there is a cold, dry season that begins in April and lasts through August. For maybe five days out of the year, the temperature drops below freezing. During the hottest months, December and January, the temperature frequently goes up as high as 102 degrees Fahrenheit.

When Magdalena arrives at one of the two reservations in northern Paraguay where the Aché now live, she has a two-mile walk to camp.

When the Aché first met Magdalena in September 1981, they were very curious. They immediately came over and touched her. They smiled and giggled. They already knew Kim from his earlier work with them, and they wanted to know if Magdalena was his girlfriend. "The Aché thought I was too skinny," she says. They also wondered why she did not have a baby. By the time most Aché girls are in their early twenties, they have at least one baby. The Aché called Magdalena "daregi" (dah-REG-ee), which means "young maiden" or "inexperienced girl."

At the end of her first month in the field with the Aché, she went on her first foraging trip, a trek into the forest to find food. During the next eight months, she would go on nine foraging trips.

The first trip was the hardest. "Getting the trust of the people

✌ The truck can't get through a flooded road, so the researchers have to walk to reach the Aché reservation.

~ Tinamou eggs are among the many different kinds of bird eggs that the Aché like to eat.

on that first foraging trip was so important," she says. "I wondered whether I would really get to the point where the Aché would trust me and understand my intentions, which were to study their behaviors in ways that would not cause them any harm. I always hoped that what I studied or my presence in their community could ultimately be of help to them in some way."

The first foraging trip was a huge test for Magdalena. Magdalena was testing herself, and the Aché were testing her. She wondered constantly whether she would be able to pass the tests. Kim had told her the foraging trip would last about two weeks. She worried whether she would be able to do all the work she was expected to do. Would she be able to keep up with the strong, physically fit Aché? Would she be able to eat their food and drink water from streams? What would happen if she got sick?

The night before they left the reservation, Magdalena packed her backpack with a few clothes, three changes of underwear, a rain poncho, and supplies such as notebooks, pens, matches, and a flashlight. She cut a sheet in half so she would not have to lie on the bare ground. Since she is a nibbler and likes to eat throughout the day, she counted out two pieces of candy for each night they would be gone and also brought a bag of peanuts. Her luxury items were some strong coffee she likes very much and a can to heat water for the coffee. She also packed medicines—aspirin, antibiotics, and antidiarrheal medication—just in case anyone got sick on the trip.

The Aché also packed their belongings. The women filled huge woven baskets called "burden baskets" with clothes, sleeping mats, fans, machetes, axes, knives, metal cooking pots, spoons, and a few food items. Each woman carries a heavy basket on her back. Women with infants carry their babies and sometimes their pet peccaries, coatis (raccoonlike animals), or monkeys in addition to the baskets. The women carry all the family's belongings. Men carry their bows and arrows, and some carry children.

Early the next morning, they set out for the forest. First there was the three-hour walk in the hot tropical sun from the reservation into the forest. Magdalena wore her notebook around her neck and carried her backpack. "I had no idea what I was doing, and the Aché knew I didn't know what I was doing," she says. "Kim was gone with the men, and I stayed behind with the women and children. I was clueless about what I was doing."

Fortunately, an older Aché woman named Japegi took a liking to Magdalena and stayed close by her. Although Magdalena didn't yet know the language well enough to talk to the woman, they managed to communicate with gestures. "She would make sure I didn't go off the trail. She would tell me to watch the ground and not to step on snakes."

꙳ Aché women carry much heavier loads than men carry.

29

~: Sometimes the Aché have to walk through a swamp or meadow to get to another part of the forest, where they hunt.

The trail that the men cut is often difficult to see, and it rarely follows a straight line. Sometimes the only clue to the trail is a few cut twigs or bent leaves. The Aché have keen eyesight and can see the tiniest detail. They have learned to be observant from childhood because the forest holds many dangers. The jaguar is the most feared animal in the forest. The Aché tell stories of relatives eaten by jaguars. They train their children to be quiet on the trail by telling them that if they make noise a jaguar may get them. The jaguar is the Aché's bogeyman.

There are other dangers, too—poisonous snakes called bothrops, with venom that can kill a person. There are thorns, bee stings, spider bites, and caterpillars that cause pain from a mere touch. In the forest, people learn to be alert and observant because their lives depend on it.

As she tried to keep up, Magdalena felt that the Aché women were just waiting to see how long it took before she got caught in vines or lost the trail entirely. And, of course, it happened.

Once when she left the group to relieve herself, she could not find the trail again. Wondering how she would ever find her way back, Magdalena suddenly realized she was not alone. A seven-year-old girl took her hand and led Magdalena back to the trail. It was one of many times over the years that Aché children have helped her.

A major test was crossing a deep stream. The Aché cut a tree and let it fall across the stream like a bridge. The tree trunk was wet and slippery, and Magdalena had to walk across it carrying her backpack. The Aché gave instructions, but because she did not understand the language, Magdalena had to observe carefully and try to follow what they did. The Aché used a long stick to balance themselves while walking across the felled tree. After crossing, they reached back to pass the stick to the next person just before stepping off the tree and onto the ground. Magdalena made it across safely, but another researcher accidentally threw the stick into the water. The Aché laughed and scolded him for not paying attention. "Until the people accept you and trust you, you're always on stage when you're doing fieldwork in the forest," Magdalena says.

᠅ Crossing a stream is tricky and requires good balance.

After many years of fieldwork, she has now been on enough foraging trips to know that although no two days are alike, there are certain patterns in the Aché's foraging behavior. She and Kim have measured the distances the people walk. As they hunt, men travel between 6 to 8.4 miles per day. The women walk about 1.2 to 2.4 miles per day.

As the women follow the trail, they take rest stops and go off to gather fruit or insects. Rest stops, which can be as short as twenty minutes or as long as two hours, are the younger children's playtime, always under the close watch of an adult or a teenage girl or boy. The children have no toys, but they use large seeds as marbles, or they pretend they are going on hunts like their fathers. They like to swing on vines and play in streams. But they have to be careful. Sometimes children fall into swiftly flowing rivers and drown.

Children also help the women forage. Girls and boys as young as five and six years old know how to collect ripe fruits. Older children climb trees and knock fruit down to the women. Since they are taught to share from an early age, the children constantly give fruit to Magdalena. Still, she had food anxieties throughout the foraging trip and worried about getting enough to eat. When she went off on her own to tend to bathroom needs, she sometimes sneaked a piece of her candy and ate it.

~ Left: Older children take care of younger ones. Right: Like children everywhere, the Aché children make up games and use whatever they find as toys.

In the late afternoon, some of the women collected palm starch, one of the main foods in the Aché diet. There are several species, or kinds, of palm trees in the forest. Finding palms that have starch takes knowledge and skill. When the women find the right kind of palm, they chop it down with metal axes, which have replaced the old stone axes they once used.

∿ Left: Japegi, Magdalena's adoptive Aché mother, enjoys a snack of palm starch. Right: Palm fiber looks like dry grass, but it tastes good.

At the top of the palm is the heart, a tender shoot rich in calcium. After cutting out the palm heart, they may eat it on the spot or save it for later. Sometimes they cook the palm heart with meat to make soup. They cut open the palm trunk and use the back of their axes to pound the fiber, or starch, inside. On a good day, the women may cut down several palms and collect forty or fifty pounds of starch. Women and children eagerly suck on the palm starch, finally satisfying their hunger pangs and moving on.

As they follow the trail, the women pick up animals that the men have killed and left behind on the ground. Throughout the day, they hear the men calling back and forth, telling each other where they are and which animals they have found. When a hunter kills an animal, he calls out and lets everyone know. "There's a monkey on the ground. I just killed it. Put it in the basket." Monkey and armadillo are favorite meats.

If the men happen to find a large beehive, they gather the honeycombs to take back to camp. Sometimes they use smoldering firewood to smoke out the bees. Other times, they chop down the tree with the hive to harvest the honey. Some of the men always get stung.

Honey is like candy for the Aché, and everyone loves to eat it. They put a piece of the waxy comb in their mouths, suck out the

～ Bepurangi uses an ax and a firebrand to collect honey.

honey, and spit out the wax. The first time the Aché offered Magdalena a piece of honeycomb, she thought she was supposed to eat everything, wax and all. Once again, the Aché laughed at her ignorance.

Deciding where to set up camp for the night involves a lot of calling back and forth between the women and men. Older women, who leave their children with relatives on the reservations, stay closer to the men and bring information back to the women with babies and small children, who have to move more slowly. When they finally decide where to set up camp, the women gather firewood.

Most often, the women set up camp near a stream or river so it will be easy to get water. The people prefer flat ground, and they like to camp near the area where they plan to forage the next day. Once they decide on a camping spot, each woman makes a fire for herself and her husband. All adult Aché women are married, and most have children. Older people travel with their grown children and help to take care of their grandchildren. On her first trip, Magdalena knew she was expected to make a fire for herself and Kim, but she didn't know how to collect firewood, so she sat and watched the others. The women go into the forest and find a dead tree. Then they cut down the entire tree or chop off huge branches, which they bring back to camp. Aché

～ The Aché eat honey straight from the honeycomb.

❧ Magdalena with Berembogi, another Aché woman who helped her in the forest. With them are Berembogi's daughter, Chachupurangi, and her children.

women are very strong and muscular and can carry large pieces of wood. Magdalena is a small, slender person and cannot carry such heavy loads.

"I would go into the forest and spend hours getting these tiny pieces of firewood. Half the time I would come back with the wrong kind of wood, and the Aché would laugh and say, 'Oh, you don't know how to get firewood.'" Then Magdalena's self-appointed protector, Japegi, the woman she now considers her Aché mother, would come over and help her build a fire. Sometimes the children helped her. The Aché use matches, which they bring from the reservation or get from Magdalena and Kim. But they don't rely on matches. After the first night in the forest, some Aché women carry in one of their hands a firebrand—a small log covered on one end with live coals from the previous night's fire.

Evening is the best part of the day for the Aché. The women remove the animals' innards and throw them on the fire. Then they cook the cleaned animals by boiling them in large metal pots or roasting them on sticks. At last they eat a real meal. For the men who have been hunting for about seven hours, this is their only real meal of the day. All the people are tired and hungry, and they stuff themselves. If the day's hunting and gathering have been good, there is plenty to eat. If not, the people share whatever they have so that no one goes without food.

After the evening meal, the Aché joke, laugh, and sing songs

~: Roasted tatu, or armadillo, is a favorite food.

After a long day of hunting and gathering, the ground feels good. The Aché mother on the left sleeps sitting up. Women who are still nursing sleep in this position. that tell stories about their lives. The fires burn throughout the night to keep the people warm and dry. Everyone beds down on the ground. The Aché sleep on mats that the women have woven from palm leaves. There are no tents, no privacy, just the comfort of one another and the darkening embrace of the forest.

New Life in an Old World

❧ "The rewards of doing anthropology are the people. I feel I have lots of Aché families. Because I'm in such a privileged situation as an anthropologist, I have more intense relationships with these people than with most other people I know except for my own family."

THE AÇHÉ LOVE BABIES, and Magdalena's relationship with these people changed on her second trip into the field, when she and Kim returned with their first daughter, Karina, then a baby of only thirteen months. Now that Magdalena had a baby, the Aché accepted her as a woman. She was no longer *daregi*—an inexperienced girl. Now she was *kuja γma* (koo-JAH ee-uu-MAH), a woman. Her coming back indicated to the Aché that she really cared for them as human beings and not just as objects to study or exploit. Also, her language skills had improved, and she could communicate better.

There is no word in the Aché language for marriage, but the people recognize that some relationships are more permanent than love affairs. Women refer to "my husband," and men refer to "my wife."

In contrast to some cultures in which marriages are arranged by parents, Aché men and

women choose their own mates. Girls in particular have a high degree of choice about potential partners. Marriage takes place either when a woman goes to sleep at a man's campfire or when a man asks a woman if he can stay with her at her campfire and she says yes.

Both men and women usually have several marriages and several divorces. A divorce occurs when one partner simply leaves the other.

Most Aché women have their first baby around the age of nineteen years and their last baby around the age of forty-two. Since they do not use birth control, Aché women may have as many as twelve children.

Until the late 1970s, when the Aché moved into houses on the reservations, women gave birth in forest camps. Today most Aché babies are born at home, but one day a baby was born in the back of Kim and Magdalena's truck. Their younger daughter, Daisha, then about nine years old, was also in the truck, and she will never forget the excitement. The baby was late, and Kim was driving the mother and two midwives—skilled people who help the mother give birth—to a small clinic in the village of Ygatimi. "The road was really bumpy," Daisha recalls. "Then they said the baby's head came out, and my dad stopped the truck."

Daisha didn't see the actual birth, but she saw the baby as

soon as it was born. Kim cut the baby's umbilical cord, an act that made him one of the baby's godparents. "Since my dad cut the cord, that made me its godsister, and it was really special," Daisha says.

As a Western child, Daisha was fortunate to be present at a baby's birth, but this isn't unusual for an Aché child. Aché parents involve their children in every aspect of life—foraging, food-sharing, happy times, sad times, birth, sickness, and death. Adults talk freely about everything in front of children, so the children grow up understanding what they will face as adults.

Every Aché baby has several jaɾɣ (ja-RUH), or godparents: the man or woman who cuts the baby's umbilical cord, the woman who bathes the baby after birth, and other adults who hold the baby soon after birth. God-parents are important for Aché children. The more godparents a child has, the more protection he or she probably has in case anything happens to one of the parents. Godparents act as extra parents for children, helping to care for them, giving advice, and teaching them how to live in their world.

Magdalena is the godmother of two Aché children. In one case, she took care of the mother and the baby after its birth. In the second case, she was called to the hut of a woman having a baby.

Inside the woman's hut were the two older men who acted as midwives. Aché women often have men as midwives, but usually the father is not present. The Aché believe that when a man's baby is born, he becomes extremely attractive to animals. For a hunter, this is good,

Kim and Daisha bury the placenta from the birth that took place in the back of their truck. The placenta is the organ inside the mother's body that nourishes a baby before it is born. After the baby is born, the placenta, which is sometimes called the afterbirth, comes out.

because it means that he may kill more animals to eat. But it may also be dangerous if he attracts an animal, such as jaguar, that could kill him.

When the baby girl was born, one of the men put it on Magdalena's lap and then cut the cord. "It was such a beautiful baby," Magdalena says. "She's my goddaughter. The whole experience was emotionally overwhelming for me as I had never been asked to attend a woman giving birth."

When a baby is born, it is given the name of an animal that the mother cooked during pregnancy. It is easy to understand why the Aché name their babies after forest animals. Animals are extremely valuable because they are the main source of food.

☙ Magdalena with the baby Warukugi, her goddaughter, and Pirajugi, the baby's mother.

Tatu, the Aché word for armadillo, a favorite food, is often the basis of a common name, Tatugi. Other popular names are Chevugi, for tapir; Japegi, for alligator; Javagi, for jaguar; Takuangi or Pwaagi, for monkey; Membogi, for snake; Chachugi, for white-lipped peccary; and Buachugi, for deer. Some names, such as Tatugi, can be for a boy or a girl. Others are different, like Takuangi for a boy and Pwaagi for a girl.

The Aché gave Magdalena, Kim, and their daughters Aché names. Magdalena's Aché name is Kajaminigi. It means little spotted cat, which the Venezuelans call cunaguaro. The name is special to Magdalena because the cunaguaro was her favorite wild animal when she was growing up in Venezuela.

Kim's Aché name is *Kanegi*, which means ornate hawk eagle. Their older daughter, Karina, is named *Atagi*, meaning rabbit. By the time Daisha was born, Magdalena and Kim decided to give her an Aché name themselves. Daisha's Aché name is *Bekrorogi*, a catfish found throughout the rivers in Latin America. Magdalena chose the name *Bekrorogi* because she had often enjoyed eating that fish when she was pregnant with Daisha during a field session with the Hiwi, a group of hunter-gatherers who live in Venezuela and Colombia.

Aché men and women love children and spend a lot of time with them. The mothers carry their babies in slings so they can nurse whenever they get hungry. Even when they sleep, nursing mothers hold their babies close to protect them. When the Aché lived only in the forest, a mother nursed her baby for about three years, but this has changed. Since the Aché began living on reservations, they may nurse only one or two years, until they become pregnant again.

Left: A pet tapir, an animal commonly found in the forest. Right: A membo pira is one of many kinds of snakes in the forest.

～ Left: Aché mothers stay close to their babies, but everyone helps to care for them, including godmothers like Chejugi. Right: Magdalena wears the pelt of a cunaguaro, her Aché name animal, around her neck.

For infants, nursing is the most important source of food because mother's milk is the most nutritious. This is true for babies everywhere. Antibodies in the mother's milk help to protect the infant from diseases. Since there is no such thing as baby food in the forest, Aché mothers chew solid food to soften it and then give it to older babies. This gets them ready to eat solid food on their own.

Mothers constantly try to protect their infants from the bugs

that are everywhere. Many times throughout the day, mothers pick tiny insects from their babies' hair and faces. They swat mosquitoes and the tiny no-see-ums that are always present. Insect bites can be dangerous. Mosquitoes carry an organism that causes malaria. Not much is known about other diseases that forest insects might carry. This is something Magdalena would like to find out.

Head lice are just a normal part of life in the forest for both adults and children. Mothers and fathers groom their children and each other by picking off head lice. When children come back to camp after foraging, the mothers immediately pick off ticks and lice. Grooming is a way of caring for one another. Magdalena knew she had really been accepted by the Aché when one of the women grabbed her head and began grooming her.

Aché men and women begin teaching their children how to live in the forest at an early

People pick head lice off one another whenever they stop to rest.

age. Most children can recognize animal tracks, identify birds from their songs, and know when fruit is ripe enough to eat. They learn which insects and plants are harmful and which ones are safe to eat. They know when meat is cooked well done and when it is too pink, or rare, to eat.

Mothers teach young girls how to soften palm leaves over a fire and weave strips of the leaves into baskets and sleeping mats. Both young girls and boys learn to take care of babies. Girls especially spend a lot of time babysitting for their mothers or other women. Men teach the boys how to make bows and arrows and how to track animals, preparing them for the day when they will become hunters.

When boys and girls reach the ages of eight to twelve, they become independent of their parents and often sleep at a neighbor's hearth in the forest or at a neighbor's house on the reservation. Sometimes teenage boys go off to live on a different reservation, but girls usually live with their parents until they marry.

"Young children are taught that stinginess is the worst trait a person can have," Magdalena says. "The sharing that goes on between the Aché kids is amazing compared to what we see in our society."

The Aché share food among the entire group. All hunters, no

∾ Tykuanangi gives her baby sister, Chengygi, a piggyback ride. Today, young girls take care of babies more often than in the past because women are having infants closer together.

matter how successful, give up their kills to be shared. They also share honey and plant and insect foods, but in a different way. A woman usually gives more of the food she collects to her husband and children than she gives to other members of the group. Women with very young children may also save some meat from the evening meal to give to their hungry children the next morning.

Each time Magdalena goes foraging with the Aché, the children always give her some of the fruits and insects they collect. One day, when she and Daisha are on a foraging trip with

〜 Left: Karina's adoptive Aché father, Bepurangi, teaches her how to shoot an arrow. Right: Grandfather Bywangi pounds palm fruit while caring for his godchild.

Aché children share the sweet vijulla fruit.

them, Magdalena decides to test the children's willingness to share. During a rest stop, she gives one piece of candy to one child. The Aché really like candy, and there are about eight children in the group. Magdalena wonders what will happen. She watches in amazement as the children get together in a circle and pass the piece of candy around three times. Each time the candy goes around, each child takes a tiny piece.

Parents teach even the youngest children to treat one another with kindness. The Aché have strong rules about violence. "Among the Aché, it's really bad to get angry," Magdalena says. "When you interview women about what kind of men they want to marry, they say, men who are gentle, men who are not angry all the time."

The Aché especially enjoy laughing. Just as children tickle one another for fun, so do the adults. Men tickle other men, women tickle other women, and men and women tickle each other. Sometimes tickling helps to relieve tension. Once at a meeting where the men were talking about politics, Magdalena saw two of the group's leaders begin tickling each other while another man was giving a very serious speech. Nobody else paid any attention to the ticklers, and the speeches went on.

Unlike many Westerners, the Aché express their emotions easily. There is much touching and hugging, and women and men cry openly with one another. "The people are much less self-conscious than we are. They don't keep everything bottled up," Magdalena says. "They don't feel that every day of their life they have to be performing for everybody else."

Magdalena enjoys the Aché's ability to express feelings. "When I'm with them, I feel so comfortable because I can cry whenever I feel like it. It's just so much a part of their culture."

For the Aché, crying is as normal as laughing. They do not hold back their tears. The first time Magdalena experienced the ease with which people cry was during a foraging trip in the early years of her fieldwork. "All of a sudden the women stopped and sat down and started crying and singing at the same time. I had no idea what was going on, and I had goosebumps all over. It was heart-wrenching. Whatever they were feeling was so deep. They were just sitting down, and there was a bunch of dead peccaries in front of them. What was so amazing about that experience was that they all stopped crying at the same time, as if somebody said, 'Okay, stop.' It was over. No sobbing. They were laughing as if nothing had happened."

Later, Magdalena learned that a dead animal may remind someone of a dead loved one who was named for that animal. Perhaps the woman who started the crying remembered a husband or a father named *Chachugi*, for peccary.

༄ Daisha and her friends share a roasted armadillo.

49

Daisha and her best Aché friend, Japegi.

Crying is also a big part of greeting and saying goodbye to close friends. Now that the Aché accept Magdalena, Kim, and their daughters as friends, the people cry with them whenever they arrive and whenever they leave the reservation. "When you leave them, they cry and cry, and you hug each other and cry," Magdalena says.

She admits that the crying sessions can be exhausting, but they're also a great way to relieve stress. She finds it remarkable that Westerners bottle up their emotions so much that they sometimes become mentally ill and have to pay for therapy that allows them to express strong feelings as openly and freely as the Aché do all the time.

THE FUTURE

∿ "These people are really undergoing the process of extinction unless we intervene in some major way. Then you wonder how you're going to intervene and whether you're going to succeed. You talk and talk and talk and talk, and you go away and wonder, Did that matter? And it does. But it takes a long time to see the payoffs."

THE AÇHÉ, LIKE ALL hunter-gatherers, are important because they are the last living clue to the ancient past of all people on Earth today. By studying the Aché, Magdalena is learning more about all of us. But although the Aché can teach us a lot about our past, they face a difficult and uncertain future. They are caught in an incredibly complex transition between the Stone Age and the Space Age.

The transition began with what anthropologists call "first contact." First contact with the modern world occurred at different times for different groups of Aché, but for the groups that Magdalena and Kim study, it began around 1970. By then, some Aché who were already living on reservations had gone into the forest to locate others who they knew were in danger of being attacked by Paraguayan peasants in the area. Already

∿ Bywangi cooks meat under a shelter of palm branches.

⤳ Aché men get ready to defend their land.

many Aché had been killed or terrorized by the peasants, and, fearing for their lives, they moved out of the forests and onto missions run by missionaries.

First contact had a staggering effect on many Aché who became ill with pneumonia and other respiratory diseases. Kim, along with missionaries, provided medical treatment and food to some Aché for several months. Eventually, most of these people who received treatment recovered, but almost half the Aché population that did not receive proper medical care died from epidemics during the 1960s and 1970s.

Once the Aché moved into reservations, their lives changed forever. They were treated like second-class citizens without any rights. Their land was taken from them and turned over to lumbering and cattle ranching industries. The Aché went from living in the open forest to living in makeshift huts with palm-thatch roofs. They continued to hunt and gather in the surrounding forests, but they also began to grow gardens. As time passed, they became more and more dependent on their gardens and less so on foraging. The houses in which they now live were built with grant money from the United States Agency for International Development (USAID).

Through the efforts of Magdalena, Kim, and a conservation-minded Paraguayan named

Raúl Gauto, a large tract of forest that formerly belonged to the Aché was purchased by a group of organizations that help to save valuable habitats and species all over the world. To protect the Aché and take care of this land, which is now known as the Mbaracayú Reserve, Raúl founded the *Fundación Moisés Bertoni*, a Paraguayan conservation organization.

In 1991, the Paraguayan Congress granted Mbaracayú legal status as a nature reserve. The law grants the Aché the right to continue hunting and gathering in the reserve as long as they use traditional methods. The law also says that the Aché will be allowed to participate in the protection and administration of the reserve and that they will be offered permanent jobs that come about as a result of scientific studies. Officials of *Fundación Moisés Bertoni*, Magdalena, Kim, and the Aché are working together to achieve these goals.

Although some Aché still return to the forest for several weeks to pursue their old way of life, they can never go back to the past. Their hunter-gatherer lifestyle is coming to an end. They are becoming more dependent on money, medicines, food, tools, and other products from the outside world. In the short amount of time since first contact, they are struggling to make changes that took our ancestors many thousands of years to make.

Between 5,000 and 10,000 years separate us from our hunter-gatherer ancestors. At around the time of 8500 B.C., some people learned how to plant crops, domesticate animals,

Some Aché now live in houses with wooden floors.

~: The old technology — a stone ax.

and farm. This seems like a very long time ago, but it is only a flicker when you consider that our species—Homo *sapiens*—is about 150,000 years old and that the earliest human ancestors appeared in Africa about 4.5 million years ago. All of the advances that affect how we live today, which we take for granted, are very very young.

Within the twentieth century, change took place faster than at any other time in the entire long stretch of human evolutionary history. People invented incredible machines and went from traveling by horse and carriage to flying in jet planes. Today we send rockets to Mars, Jupiter, and the reaches of deep space. In the past few decades, computer technology has revolutionized communications and united the planet in cyberspace. Scientists have decoded the basic recipe for life. Even for many of us who have grown up with new technology, life moves faster and faster.

But for the Aché, that speed of change is unimaginable. In just one generation, they have been forced to leap over all those thousands of years, from hunting and gathering to farming with tractors, wearing shoes and clothes, living in houses, and learning about telephones, television, VCRs, computers, cars, trucks, airplanes, cities, hospitals, schools, and politics. They have even learned to play soccer, and they now compete with other teams.

As they struggle to learn how to farm and adapt to a more settled life, the Aché are suffering from many new problems with which they are not equipped to cope. Since their contact with the outside world, tuberculosis, a disease they never had in the forest, has struck them,

causing a great deal of suffering, weight loss, and inability to work. In 1994, tuberculosis became an epidemic throughout the Aché groups that Magdalena and Kim study. They helped doctors test every Aché for the disease. Then the doctors gave medicine to those who had tuberculosis. They saved many lives.

The Aché are also coming down with malaria, another disease they seldom had in the forest. When it rains on the reservations, puddles of water stand in the fields, providing breeding places for mosquitoes that carry malaria.

Since the Aché began farming, their diet has gotten worse. In the forest, they ate a variety of meats, insects, fresh fruits, and other plant foods. On the farms, they cultivate one main crop—manioc, a starchy root that is an important food in tropical America. Although Aché families keep a few domesticated animals such as pigs and chickens, they are not

Left: Farming, the new way of life. Men clear land to plant manioc. Right: An Aché farmer drives the new tractor donated by Magdalena.

~ Aché farmers grow corn, which is now replacing some of the foods they ate in the forest.

eating as much meat as they did in the forest. As a result of the lack of protein, vitamins, and variety in their diet, the Aché are suffering from malnutrition. Because they are not getting as much exercise, they have lost muscle strength. Women are not nursing as long and the children are becoming malnourished and sick. Women are suffering from many pregnancies so close together.

The Aché's health is also threatened by serious sanitation problems on the reservations. In the forest, the Aché never stayed near their waste for more than two days. Now, in the settlements, they live in the midst of waste—not only human waste but also that of their farm animals. The people clean up the waste as best they can and have built latrines, or outdoor toilets made by digging holes in the ground, but the region is so wet that the latrines quickly fill with water and collapse.

The constantly increasing waste contains enormous numbers of parasites that infect people and cause diarrhea and other bad intestinal diseases. "It's a public health problem that I'll probably be working on for the rest of my life," Magdalena says.

FOLLOWING IN HER mother's footsteps, Magdalena has learned more about immunology and epidemiology—the study of birth, death, and disease in a large population. Contrary to the commonly held belief that hunter-gatherers' lives are short, Magdalena and Kim have learned that at least a third of all Aché live to age sixty—about the same life expectancy as that of other rural people in developing countries.

Magdalena has found that the Aché seem to have a remarkable immune system. As long as they remain in their own environment and do not come in contact with other people, they will not have many health conditions that people in Western countries have. It is very unusual to see Aché with asthma or high blood pressure. Magdalena

~: Magdalena and Bywangi, an Aché health-care worker, count tuberculosis pills.

does not know of any case of diabetes among the Aché she studies. Their immune systems are very different from those of people in the United States, Japan, or Europe. Magdalena and a team of medical researchers are trying to learn why.

To provide ongoing medical care for the Aché, Magdalena has already trained one Aché health-care worker who can take health histories, diagnose common illnesses, and give out medicines. Magdalena hopes to set up clinics for the Aché and the Paraguayan peasants who live in the region. She plans to bring microscopes so she can teach people about germs and parasites and the importance of using soap, washing their hands, wearing shoes, and using latrines.

 Magdalena and Kim's new research station in the Mbaracayú Forest Reserve

Although the Aché have many needs in making the transition to a new way of life, health is a top priority. Without good medical care and better sanitation, the Aché don't have a chance.

After many years of studying the Aché, Magdalena and Kim feel a great debt of gratitude to the people for accepting them into their community and enabling them to do field studies. Now Magdalena and Kim want to give back as much as they can. To help the Aché they have set up a foundation called the Native Peoples and Tropical Conservation Fund. Their goals are ambitious. In addition to training Aché in conservation management and health care, they want to bring in computers and a team of educators to improve the schools. The Aché need to learn Spanish, and they need training in skills to care for and eventually manage the Mbaracayú Reserve. They also need skills to help them succeed in the new market economy in which they now struggle to live.

For those who argue that anthropologists should leave hunter-gatherers in a pristine environment, Magdalena points out that the moment contact is made, there is no longer any pristine environment. When hunter-gatherers make contact, they become part of an international community that recognizes basic human rights, such as freedom and good health. Magdalena feels it would be irresponsible and unethical not to help the Aché become aware that they have rights. "If we have the know-how and the ability, we have to do something," she says. "We do make a difference."

The key, Magdalena believes, is educating people to understand how biology and ecology influence all our lives. With understanding, people can give up our fear of differences and develop trust. We can reach out and care for one another as members of the same human species.

᠃ Magdalena and Daisha with Koaregi, an artist who makes wooden sculptures. Koaregi is one of the Aché who contracted tuberculosis and became unable to hunt or work in the fields. Now he tries to make a living by selling his artwork to tourists.

🌀 Tykuanangi with his son Bywangi. Aché fathers spend a lot of time with their children.

WHAT YOU CAN DO TO HELP

If you would like to help the Aché, you can make a tax-free contribution to

Native Peoples and Tropical Conservation Fund

c/o A. Magdalena Hurtado, Ph.D.

Associate Professor

Department of Anthropology

University of New Mexico

Albuquerque, NM 87131

Telephone: 505-277-4524

www.unm.edu/~kimhill/NPTC/home.html

Checks should be made payable to

Native Peoples and Tropical Conservation Fund/UNM Foundation

Tax ID # 85-0275408

A. Magdalena Hurtado and Kim Hill are donating their share of
the proceeds from the sale of this book to the Aché.

∾ Aché children love to laugh and tickle one another.

WHAT IT TAKES TO BE
AN ANTHROPOLOGIST

∾ Aché children have helped Magdalena out of many a tight spot. Once they found a retainer she had lost in the forest.

Whenever anyone asks Magdalena what it takes to be a good anthropologist, she replies that in addition to knowing biology, math, statistics, research design, ethnography, and biological anthropology, the most important thing is being interested in people. She advises young people to seek out friends from other countries in their school or neighborhood. Then they should interact with them, get to know their families, and learn about their languages and cultures.

"When I talk to people who haven't had experiences in other places, one of the things they're most fearful of is just interacting with somebody who's different. That's a big obstacle for an anthropologist. You really need to learn early on that it's not a big deal. It's really simple; all you have to do is be a courteous, empathetic, curious person."

FURTHER READING

Chagnon, Napoleon. 1992. *Yanomamo: The Last Days of Eden*. San Diego: Harcourt Brace Jovanovich.

Hill, Kim, and A. Magdalena Hurtado. 1996. *Aché Life History: The Ecology and Demography of a Foraging People*. New York: Aldine de Gruyter.

Hrdy, Sarah Blaffer. 1999. *Mother Nature: A History of Mothers, Infants, and Natural Selection*. New York: Pantheon Books.

Kroll, Virginia. 1998. *With Love: To Earth's Endangered Peoples*. Nevada City, Calif.: Dawn Publications.

Lee, Richard B., and Irven DeVore, eds. 1998. *Kalahari Hunter-Gatherers: Studies of the !Kung San and Their Neighbors*. iUniverse.com.

Shostak, Marjorie. 1983. *Nisa: The Life and Words of a !Kung Woman*. New York: Vintage Books.

꙳ The old ways of foraging in the forest. A man has just dug up a tegu lizard.

INDEX